Linking art to the world around us

Arty Facts

Machines, Transportation & Art Activities

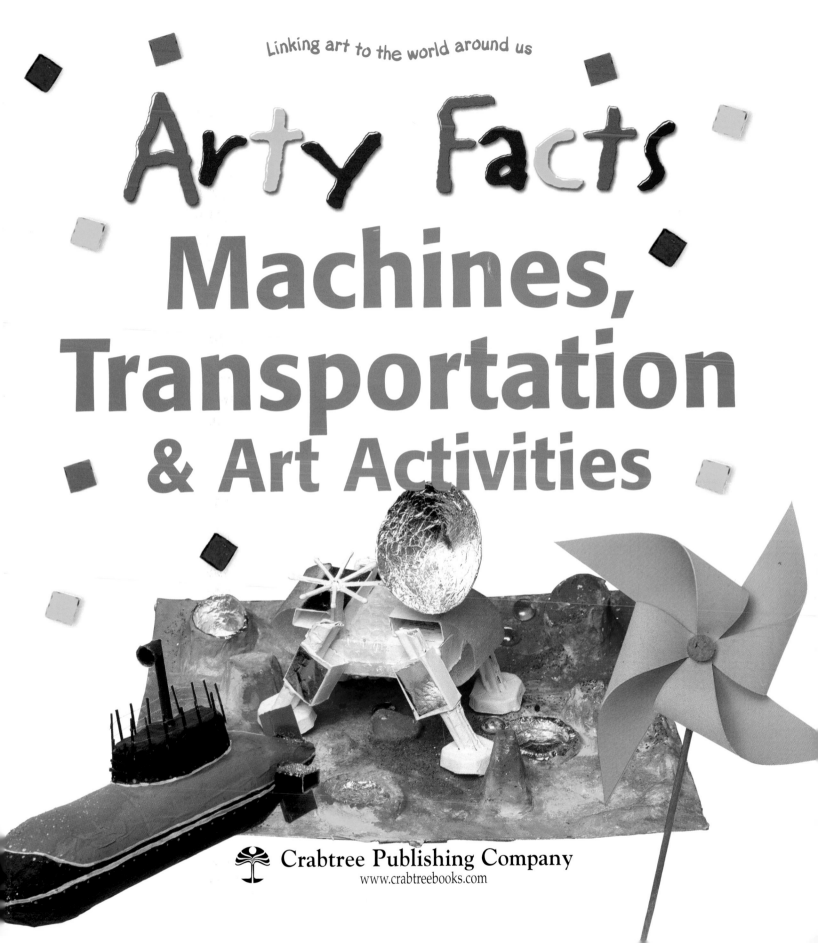

Crabtree Publishing Company
www.crabtreebooks.com

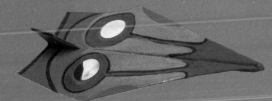

Crabtree Publishing Company

PMB 16A, 350 Fifth Avenue, Suite 3308
New York, NY
10118

612 Welland Avenue
St. Catharines, Ontario
L2M 5V6

Coordinating Editor: Ellen Rodger
Project Editor: Carrie Gleason
Production Coordinator: Rosie Gowsell

Project Development and Concept Marshall Direct:
Editorial Project Director: Karen Foster
Editors: Claire Sippi, Hazel Songhurst, Samantha Sweeney
Researchers: Gerry Bailey, Alec Edgington
Design Director: Tracy Carrington
Designers: Claire Penny, Paul Montague,
James Thompson, Mark Dempsey
Production: Victoria Grimsell, Christina Brown
Photo Research: Andrea Sadler
Illustrator: Jan Smith
Model Artist: Sophie Dean

Prepress, printing, and binding by Worzalla Publishing Company

Stringer, John, 1945-
    Machines, transportation, and art activities / written by John Stringer.
        p. cm. -- (Arty facts)
    Summary: Information about various topics related to machines, especially those
    used for transportation, forms the foundation for a variety of craft projects.
        Includes index.
    ISBN 0-7787-1116-1 (rlb) -- ISBN 0-7787-1144-7 (pb)
    1. Transportation--Juvenile literature. 2. Transportation--Study and teaching
    (Elementary)--Activity programs. [1. Transportation. 2. Machinery. 3. Handicraft.] I.
    Title. II. Series.
    TA1149 .S78 2003
    629.04--dc21

                                                        2002011630
                                                        LC

Created by
Marshall Direct Learning

© 2002 Marshall Direct Learning

FRONT COVER IMAGES: PETER MENZEL/ SCIENCE PHOTO LIBRARY; PICTOR INTERNATIONAL; NASA; TONY STONE IMAGES

Linking art to the world around us

Arty Facts

Machines, Transportation & Art Activities

Contents

WRITTEN BY John Stringer

Printing blocks

Before the **printing press** was invented, anything you wanted to copy, such as a letter or a book, had to be block-printed or copied by hand. This was a slow process. The printing press made copying easier, faster, and with fewer errors.

Printing in China

The Chinese invented block printing in the sixth century. By the late ninth century, they were printing books. To block-print, a whole page of words was carved into a wooden block then covered with ink and pressed onto paper. In 1045, the printer Bi Sheng made the first moveable type from clay. Moveable type means that each letter, or piece of type, is carved on its own block, and can be used more than once.

Gutenberg's press

Printing by machines in Europe began in 1450, with the printing press invented by the German, Johannes Gutenberg. Gutenberg's press used separate pieces of metal for each letter, which were locked into a metal frame to form a line of text. The same piece was used over and over again. Gutenberg's press printed about 300 pages a day.

New ideas

The early printing presses were worked by hand. In the 1800s a labor-saving, **steam-powered** cylinder press was made in London, England. This press used a rotating cylinder to press the paper against a flat surface that held the type. It printed over 1,000 sheets an hour. Later, rotary presses, which had type attached to the cylinder, printed 2,000 sheets an hour. Today, high-speed printing machines print in color on both sides of the paper, and are controlled by a computer. Modern printing presses that print from large **reels** of paper produce up to 60,000 copies an hour.

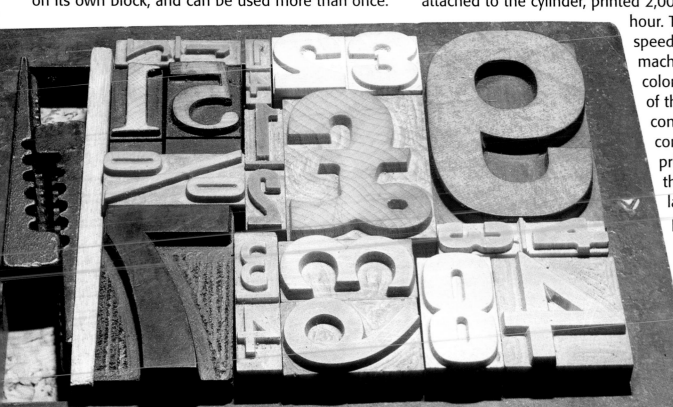

Machines

WHAT YOU NEED

potato

tissue paper

plastic knife

paints

paintbrush

scissors

gluestick

colored paper

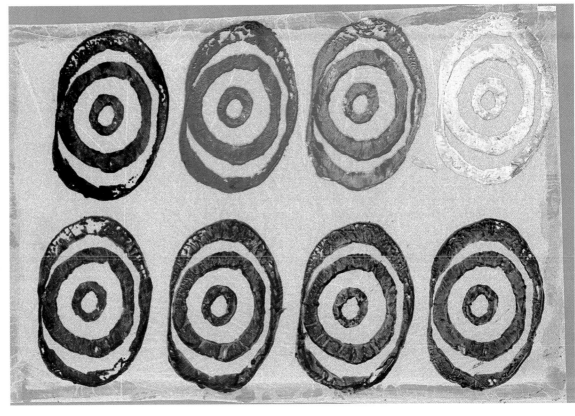

Print patterns onto paper with carrots and onions too

1 Cut a potato in half. Use the plastic knife to carve a pattern into it.

You can also make some funny face potato prints!

2 Brush paint onto the surface of the potato.

3 Press the potato onto tissue paper to make your print.

4 Cut out your tissue paper prints and mount them on colored paper.

5

Gas bags

A group of colorful balloons drifting across the sky is exciting to watch. How do the balloons get up there? The person controlling the balloon, called the balloonist, uses a steady supply of hot air to get the balloon up in the sky and to keep it in the air. Before the balloon takes off, a fire is lit under the balloon's base, heating the air inside the balloon.

Hot air

Hot-air balloons lift passengers because hot air behaves in a special way. When the air inside the balloon is heated, its invisible **molecules** move faster and begin pushing against each other. As the molecules move faster, they expand, or take up more space, filling up the room inside the balloon. The air expansion causes the balloon to inflate and rise. Molecules move around more when they are warm and less when they are cold.

Liftoff

The warm air inside the balloon is now lighter than the cooler air outside. The lighter air rises, and takes the balloon, basket, and passengers with it. The balloonist keeps the air inside the balloon warm by keeping the flame at its base burning.

Going up

Heating the air in your house will not make your house blow away, but it does make the air rise. Hot air flows toward the ceiling and spreads out. When the air cools it sinks back down toward the floor.

Transportation

Hot-air balloon

Why not add some passengers to the basket of the balloon?

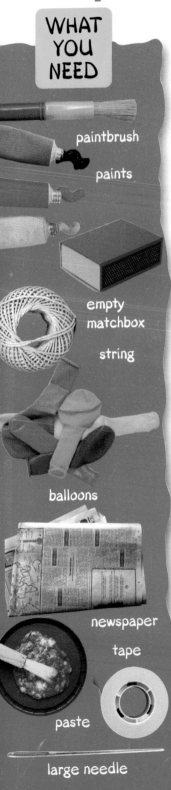

WHAT YOU NEED

paintbrush

paints

empty matchbox

string

balloons

newspaper

tape

paste

large needle

1

Blow up the balloon and tie a knot in the end.

2

Paste and cover the balloon with small strips of newspaper.

3

When dry, paint the balloon different patterns and colors. When the paint is dry, burst the balloon with the needle.

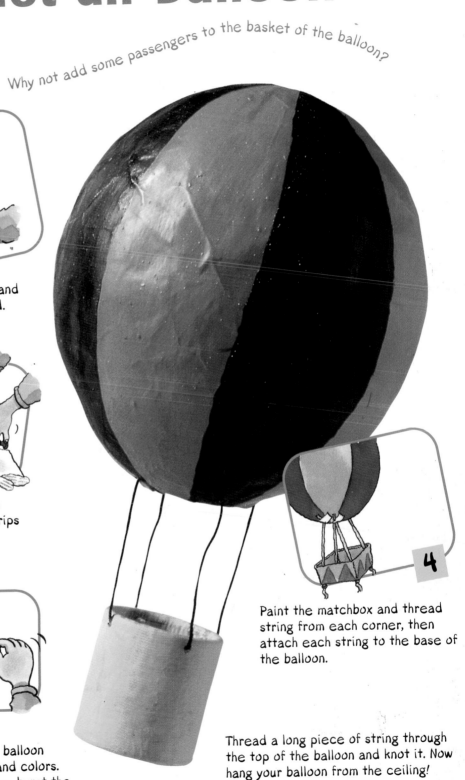

4

Paint the matchbox and thread string from each corner, then attach each string to the base of the balloon.

Thread a long piece of string through the top of the balloon and knot it. Now hang your balloon from the ceiling!

Skyrails

Monorail trains are not like the trains we usually see running along two rails on the ground. Monorail trains run along only one rail. Several countries use monorail trains. The first monorail in the United States opened at Disneyland in California in 1959. An eight-mile (13-km) rail was specially built for the 1964 Olympic Games in Tokyo, the capital city of Japan.

Fast and quiet

Monorail trains are designed to travel faster and quieter than regular trains, and to use fuel more efficiently. Some monorail trains are powered by **electric motors**, others have **gas engines**, and some use gas **turbines**. All monorail trains have guide-wheels that keep the trains in place along the rail. The guide-wheels are usually made from rubber, which make the trains quieter than regular trains.

Hanging from rails

One type of monorail train is suspended trains, which hang from a rail, or guideway, above the train. The separate wagons, known as cars, hang from the rail. The rail provides **electricity** for the cars to move, and acts as support for the guide-wheels. In newer split-rail trains, cars hang from two rails hidden inside a closed section. The closed section keeps the tracks dry and the train quieter.

Balancing on the rails

Most monorail trains run above the rail. The cars rest on, or straddle, the rail. This type of monorail uses an instrument called a **gyroscope** to balance the cars and keep them upright. The cars also have guide-wheels that grip the side of the rail.

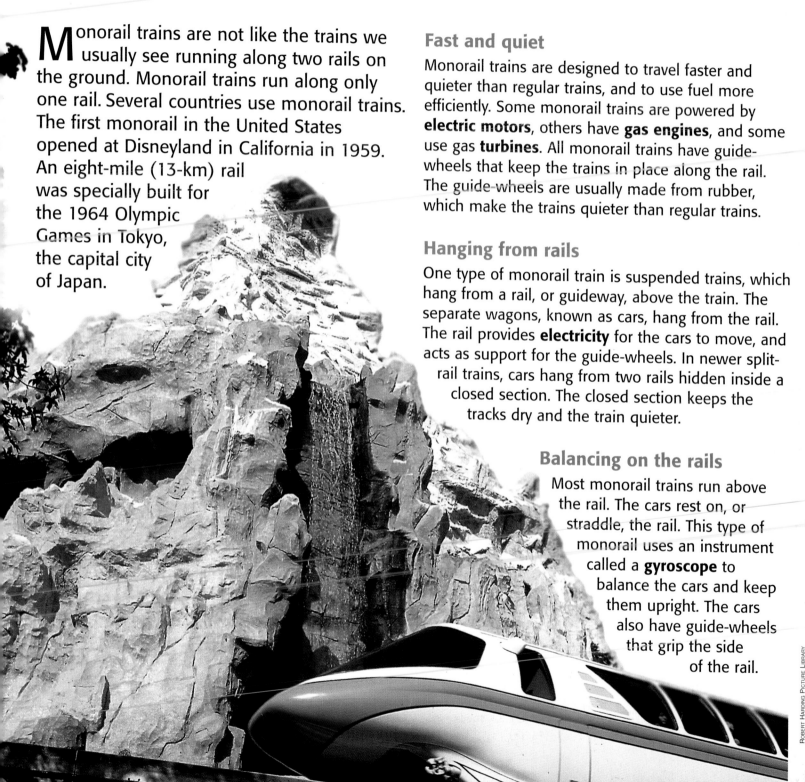

Machines

Mini monorail

You can make and operate...

WHAT YOU NEED

- small cardboard cartons
- metallic paint
- poster board
- paintbrush
- tin foil
- scissors
- beads
- buttons
- sequins
- paper shapes
- cardboard box
- glue
- wool
- tracing paper

1 Paint one of the cartons with metallic paint and cover another with tin foil.

2 Cut windows out of the side, front, and back. Glue the tracing paper inside for windows.

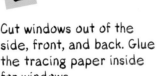

3 Decorate with sequins, beads, buttons, and paper shapes.

4 To make the wheels, glue three sequins to each side of the top of the box. Make two small tabs from poster board and glue on top of the box.

... a miniature monorail system

5 Thread two pieces of wool through the tabs on your car. Poke the ends through the cardboard box to make the monorail station. Paint in bright colors.

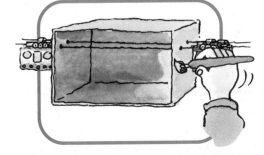

Ask an adult to run long pieces of craft wire across your room to make the rails for your monorail cars. Attach the ends of the wire to hooks screwed into walls, the ceiling, high shelves, or tall furniture.

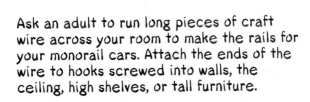

9

Steam engines

The first steam engines were used to pump water and power machines. Improved steam engines were used to power the first trains. The trains only ran a little faster than a horse, but as **engineering** improved, so did the speed of trains. By 1845, steam trains traveled at 25 miles (40 km) an hour. Fifty years later, they were running at more than twice that speed. Modern steam trains are still in use in many parts of the world and travel at more than 78 miles (125 km) an hour.

High pressure

When water boils, it becomes steam. Steam takes up more space than water, so it pushes, producing pressure. This pressure moves objects, such as the pistons on steam engines. A piston is a disk that fits tightly inside a tube or cylinder. When steam enters the cylinder at high pressure, it expands. The pressure of expanding steam on the piston pushes it up the cylinder. Holes called valves let the steam escape, and the piston moves back down the cylinder. A **rod and crank** are connected to the piston and to the train's wheels. The pushing and pulling movement of the piston in turn move the steam engine's wheels.

Boiling water

Water is usually heated by burning fuel, such as coal, in a furnace. Some modern steam engines use heat from a **nuclear reactor** to produce steam.

BRIAN SOLOMON/ MILEPOST 92 1/2

CORBIS

Machines

WHAT YOU NEED

poster board

silver buttons

popsicle sticks

toothpicks

bottle caps

nails

metallic paper

scissors

glue

pencil

brush

gold and silver paint

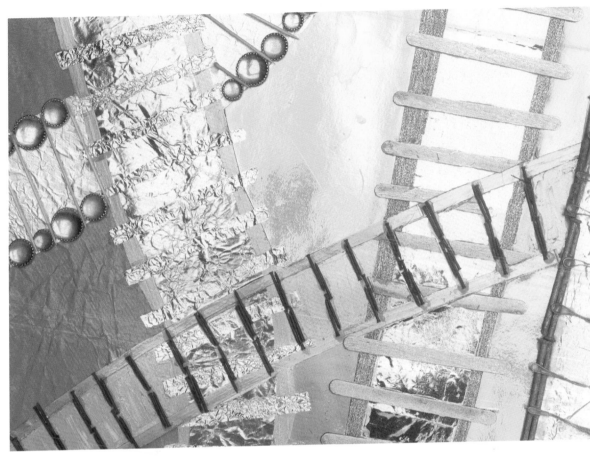

Add some model trains traveling along the tracks!

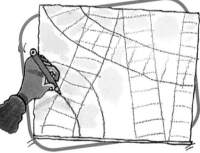

1 Draw train tracks, some crossing each other, on the poster board.

2 Fill the spaces between the tracks with pieces of metallic paper and gold and silver paint.

3 Use the nails, popsicle sticks, toothpicks, silver buttons, and bottle caps to form the train tracks.

11

Bicycles

When wheels turn, they move objects, including machines such as cars, skateboards, toys, and even giant fairground rides. A bicycle is a simple machine made of two large wheels and a frame. Bicycle wheels help you speed around town, and the only fuel you need is pedal power!

Wheels to turn wheels

A bicycle is energy efficient because it takes you a long way for little physical effort. As well as two main wheels, a bicycle has a series of smaller wheels t help it move. The pedals are attached to chainrings. Chainrings are **sprockets**, or met wheels with teeth that hold a chain. The chain is also wrapped around a series of smaller sprockets, called cogs, that are attached to the rear wheel of the bicyc If you turn the pedals once, the chainring also turns once. Every time the chainring turns once, the cogs turi twice, making the rear wheel turn twice. The rear wheel is 79 inches (200 cm) round. With one turn of the pedals, you can travel 158 inches (40(cm), or 13 feet (4 m) along the road.

Energy saver

When you shift **gears** on the bicycle, you are moving the chain from one-sized cog to another. The different-sized cogs change how much power you need to pedal. If you are goir uphill, a low gear, with the chain wrapped along larger cog, moves you forward slowly without havin to work hard.

Transportation   Wheel pattern

WHAT YOU NEED

round tapestry or picture frame

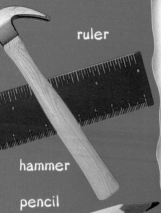

nails

colored thread

ruler

hammer

pencil

1 Use a pencil and ruler to mark 25 points at equal intervals around the sides of the frame.

2 Ask an adult to help you hammer the nails in at each point.

3 Tie a piece of thread around a nail, then wind it around the ninth or tenth nail to the right as shown.

Build up threads into a circular pattern

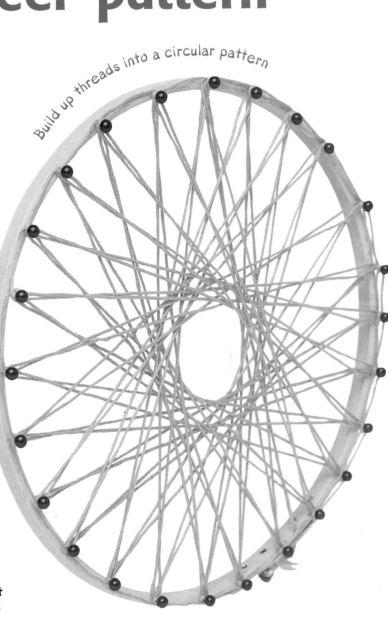

4 Bring the thread back and wind it around the nail next to the one you started with. Continue criss-crossing the thread across the frame, making spokes all the way around.

Windjammers

The windjammer, or clipper, is a large sailing ship. These ships were first built in the United States in the 1800s. They sailed from the east coast of the United States around the tip of South America to China, where they loaded up with tea and spices before returning. Windjammers were later used to carry gold mined in North America and South Africa to Europe. Smaller windjammers, called schooners, transported coal, oysters, and even Christmas trees across the ocean.

Slender and fast

A windjammer, such as the *Flying Cloud* or the *Cutty Sark*, had a narrow body, or hull, that was deeper at the back than at the front. Large sails hung from each tall **mast** to catch as much wind as possible. The windjammer was modeled on the famous Baltimore Clippers, of Chesapeake Bay in Virginia and Maryland. They were named clippers because their speed clipped so much time off the voyage.

Record breakers

At the time, windjammers were the fastest means of travel. It was not long before windjammers began to break records. The *James Baines* crossed the Atlantic Ocean in just twelve days and six hours. The *Andrew Jackson* sailed from New York, around the Cape of Good Hope in South Africa and on to San Francisco in 89 days and nine hours. The *Champion of the Seas* sailed 536 miles (862 km) in 24 hours, a record that was not matched for another 25 years.

End of an era

The Suez Canal created a new trade route when it opened in 1869. It linked the Red Sea to the Mediterranean, so windjammers were no longer needed for the tea trade. Instead, they began sailing to Australia for wool. Eventually, the wool trade needed larger ships instead of fast ones and soon the windjammers were replaced by square-riggers, which were designed to carry larger shipments at slower speeds.

Transportation

Sail sculptures

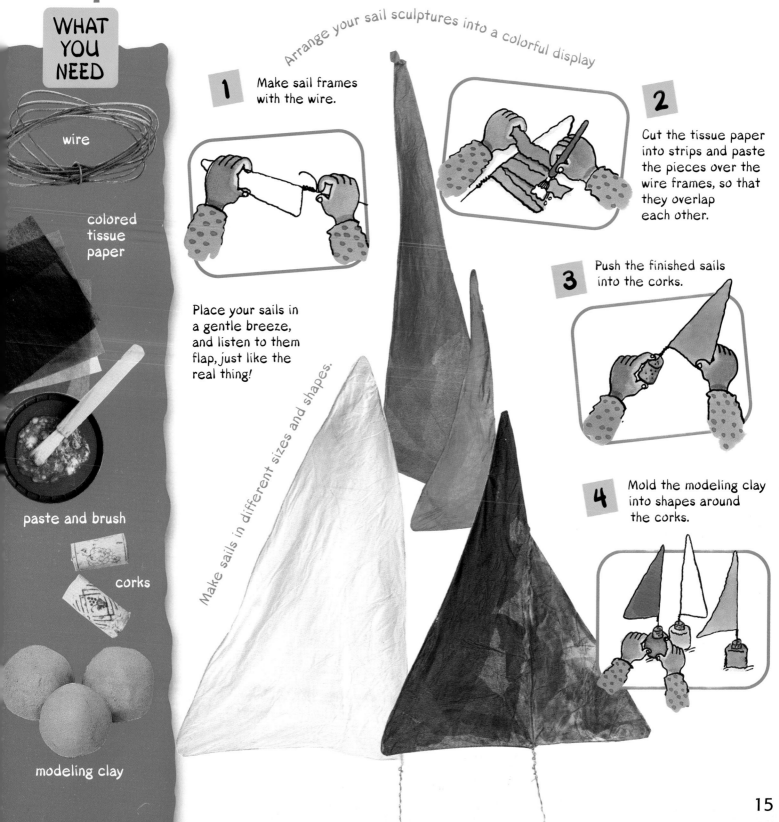

Arrange your sail sculptures into a colorful display

wire

colored tissue paper

paste and brush

corks

modeling clay

1 Make sail frames with the wire.

Place your sails in a gentle breeze, and listen to them flap, just like the real thing!

Make sails in different sizes and shapes.

2 Cut the tissue paper into strips and paste the pieces over the wire frames, so that they overlap each other.

3 Push the finished sails into the corks.

4 Mold the modeling clay into shapes around the corks.

15

Submarine

We know less about the bottom of the sea than we do about the Moon. The sea bottom is very dark and cold, making underwater travel difficult for humans.

Tons of water press down on everything deep in the ocean. The only way to explore and map the bottom of the sea is in submarines, which are underwater ships designed to resist the pressure, or weight, of the water.

Periscope-vision

Military submarines have an instrument for seeing above the water called a periscope. A periscope is a metal tube, as much as 66 feet (20 m) long, with a reflecting mirror at each end. It is mechanically operated to move up and down through the water. Above the surface, it rotates to look in a complete circle. When the submarine commander needs to know what is happening on the surface, he only needs to peer into the periscope for a full view.

Submersibles

Deep-sea vessels are called submersibles. Their ball shape spreads the pressure of the water evenly over the vessel's entire body. Torpedo-shaped submarines cannot go as deep as submersibles because the water pressure crushes them. Submersibles dive as deep as 3,300 feet (1,000 m). They have mechanical arms to collect samples from the ocean floor, and searchlights to help the crew see in the dark.

ROVs

Remote-Operated Vehicles, or ROVs, do not have a human crew. They are controlled from the surface or from a submersible and signals are sent back by a cable. ROVs go into places that are too dangerous for a crew, such as caves and shipwrecks. ROVs are also used to repair oil rigs and pipelines.

Machines

plastic bottle

newspaper

glue

bamboo stick

toothpicks

glitter

acetate

scissors

poster board

paints and brush

Mini-sub

2 Cut a circle out of poster board, make a slit, and fold into a cone shape as shown. Glue the cone to one end of the bottle.

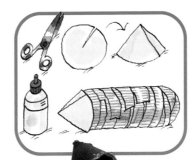

1 Glue pieces of newspaper over a large plastic bottle. Cover the whole bottle and let it dry.

3 Use poster board to make the rudder and look-out deck of the submarine. Glue them on.

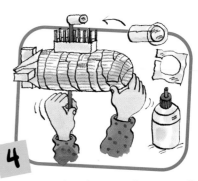

4 Insert a bamboo stick vertically through the middle of the sub. At the top, glue a piece of rolled-up poster board to make a periscope. Glue a circle of acetate at the end to make the lens. Glue toothpick rails around the top of the submarine.

Push the sub's periscope up and down and swivel it left and right!

5 Paint and decorate your submarine. Add silver glitter for a water effect.

Propellers

ROBIN ADSHEAD; THE MILITARY PICTURE LIBRARY/ CORBIS

Propellers are blades that are attached to a **turning shaft**. Placed on top or in front of a vehicle, such as an airplane or a ship, they help propel, or push, it forward.

The first propeller

The idea of how a propeller works was first introduced by an Ancient Greek scientist named Archimedes, who discovered that a turning a screw-like device raised water from a lower level to a higher one. Hundreds of years later, this idea was used to build a propeller which changed the turning power of an engine into a forward movement.

Airplane and ship propellers

Airplane and ship propellers work in the same way. Airplane propellers are known as airscrews. The turning blades produce a force called aerodynamic lift. Two or more of the blades are positioned at the angle that gives the best lift. The blades also help push or pull the vehicle through the air. Smaller aircraft have blades that are fixed. Larger aircraft propellers swivel to increase the lift, or even reverse for braking. Most ships have propellers with three or four blades. Twin-screw ships have two propellers, one turning clockwise, to the right, and one turning counter-clockwise, to the left.

Machines

Propeller barge

poster board   pencil

scissors

paints

paintbrush

ruler

glue

corrugated cardboard

small box

straw

1 Draw the shapes shown below on the piece of poster board. Cut them out and paint them.

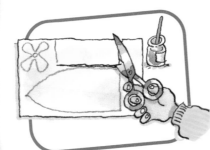

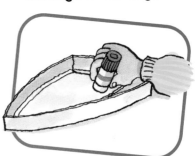

2 Cut a long, thin piece of poster board. Make notches along one edge and fold.

3 Glue this piece of poster board around the edge of the barge's base.

Fill your barge with a cargo of beads or buttons

Cut a small flap from the back of the barge and stick the engine onto it.

4 Glue the cardboard onto a small box. Cut windows out of three sides and a door out of the fourth, then paint it.

5 Make a small hole in the propeller and push the end of the straw through it.

6 Make an engine cover by notching, folding, and gluing a rectangle of poster board. Glue the propeller inside.

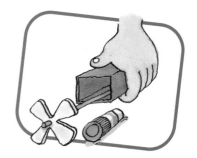

Speed up!

A fast-moving vehicle needs to be lightweight and have a powerful motor. It also has to move as easily as possible through air or water. A smooth, **streamlined** shape reduces **friction**, by letting air or water flow smoothly around the vehicle, allowing it to go faster.

Strong and light

Race cars, powerboats, and high-speed trains are all light, powerful, and streamlined. A race car is low and wide, so it moves easily through the air. The powerful engine of a Formula 1 race car is behind the driver's seat. The driver leans back in order to create as little air **resistance** as possible. The car is made from a lightweight but strong material. Its body flaps press the car down on the road, so that the tires grip better.

High-speed power

Powerboat motors spin propellers to push them along at top speed. They have streamlined hulls designed to slice through the water. High-speed trains, such as the French TGV, travel up to 186 miles (300 km) an hour. Streamlined tilting trains, which lean as they go around bends, go even faster. Made from lightweight **aluminum**, they are driven by powerful electric motors that get their electricity from cables above the track.

Transportation

WHAT YOU NEED

magazine pictures

ruler

scissors

glue

pencil

white or black poster board

Zoom pictures

Cut and glue a series of fantastic fast-moving images

1 Look through magazines and cut out pictures of cars, buses, planes, and other vehicles.

2 Use a pencil and ruler to divide the pictures into narrow slanted strips. Cut these out.

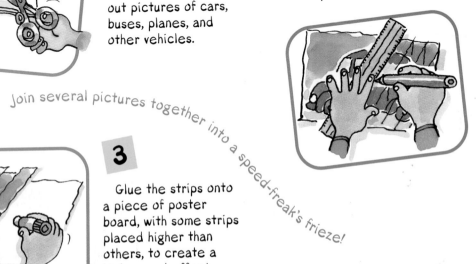

Join several pictures together into a speed-freak's frieze!

3 Glue the strips onto a piece of poster board, with some strips placed higher than others, to create a high-speed effect.

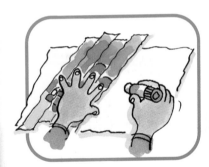

Clockworks

Clocks and watches measure and show us the time. Some watches have hands that point to numbers on a face or dial, and others have **digital** numbers that change as the seconds tick away. The parts inside work together, moving at exactly the right speed to keep the right time. Mechanical clocks and watches work because a weight falls or a **spring** unwinds. Modern clocks and watches use a different kind of energy.

Weights and springs

Inside an old-fashioned mechanical clock or pocket watch, a part called an **escapement** makes a weight fall or a spring unwind at the correct speed. This action moves the gear wheels which move the second, minute, and hour hands.

Vibrating quartz

In **quartz** clocks and watches, energy usually comes from a battery. To keep the mechanism at the right speed, the energy from the battery passes through a quartz crystal, which vibrates at exactly 32,768 pulses per second. A **microchip** slows the pulse to one pulse per second, so the clock or watch keeps perfect time. When the battery loses power, the watch stops. A **perpetual** quartz watch runs forever because a heavy, unbalanced wheel inside swings as your arm moves, driving a **generator** to make electricity. The electricity passes through a quartz crystal and a microchip and drives the mechanism.

Machines

Move the hands around the clock to tell the time. Swing the pendulum to mark the seconds!

WHAT YOU NEED

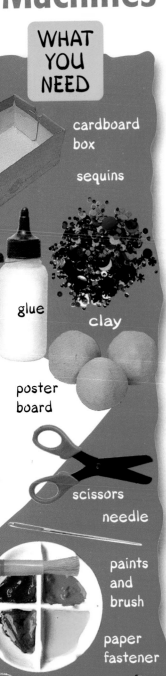

cardboard box

sequins

glue

clay

poster board

scissors

needle

paints and brush

paper fastener

gold thread

black marker   pencil

1

Draw a fun shape on poster board big enough to cover one side of the box. Cut out and glue on.

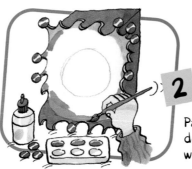

2

Paint and decorate it with sequins.

3

Use the marker to draw the face and numbers. Cut out two hands from poster board. Make holes in both hands and in the center of the face. Attach the hands with a paper fastener to the center.

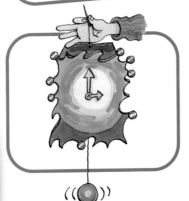

4 Make a circular pendulum from clay. Attach a piece of gold thread. When dry, paint and thread through the end of the box, securing with a knot at the top.

23

Music machines

To create a tune, or song, with loud and soft, high and low **notes**, you need a music machine, or instrument. When you touch a piano key, a system of **levers** swing soft hammers to hit tight wires of different lengths. The wire then vibrates, or moves back and forth, and you hear the note. When the hammer drops back, a soft **damper** touches the wire to stop it from vibrating. This stop-and-go action allows you to play fast, lively tunes on a piano.

Vibrations and overtones

When you play an instrument, you make a vibration. Every instrument vibrates in the same way and makes the same basic notes. What makes each instrument sound different are the **overtones**, the tiny vibrations on top of the main note.

A guitar and a violin are made in different shapes and from different materials. The overtones of a guitar are different from the overtones of a violin, so they sound different. An electronic **synthesizer** makes sounds like any other instrument, because it produces a wide range of vibrations and copies the overtones.

Electronic effects

When you press the keys of a synthesizer, it produces vibrations electronically. **Filters** in the machine let some vibrations through and stop others. This alters the sound and creates echo-like effects to add to the sounds of other instruments. You can also alter the volume of the sound and how long it lasts. Each key you press varies the amount of electricity flowing through the machine and changes the sound.

Pick-ups and amplifiers

An electric guitar has metal strings close to magnetic parts called pick-ups. A tiny electric current in the pick-ups is created when the strings vibrate, or are strummed. This electric current is the signal that goes to an amplifier, which makes the sound bigger and louder.

Machines

Cutlery chimes

WHAT YOU NEED

spoon

metal objects such as forks, knives, nails, goblets, and egg cups

toast rack

gold thread

large sequins

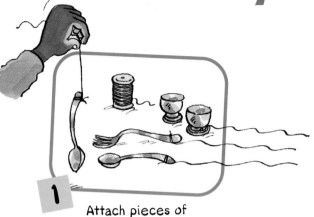

1 Attach pieces of thread around a selection of metal objects. Add sequins at points along the thread.

2 Tie all of these to the toast rack.

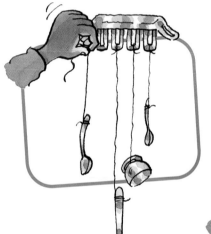

3 Attach a piece of gold thread from the toast rack and hang it from the ceiling. Use a metal spoon to strike your chimes.

Listen to the different sounds each metal object makes

Moving parts

Mechanical toys move because of the parts, or mechanisms, inside them.

These mechanisms include motors with gear wheels, as well as rods, cams, and cranks. Each part is linked to the next. Together, the parts make the wheels of a toy car turn, a model soldier move his arms to beat a drum, or a fierce toy lion open and close his mouth to swallow a lion tamer!

Wheels at work

A gear is a wheel with teeth, or cogs, around its outside rim. The cogs on one gear fit into the spaces between the cogs in another gear. When gears turn together, they move a part of a mechanism. Gears also make a movement faster or slower, stronger or weaker, or change its direction.

Racks, cams, and cranks

A rod with teeth on it is called a rack. When a gear wheel locks with a rack, it pushes the rack from side to side. The arm of a toy violinist is pushed and pulled by a rack. A cam is an irregular-shaped wheel that pushes on a rod. The shape of the cam controls the movement of the rod. As the cam turns, it pushes the rod up and down, so the neck and head of a mechanical toy move up and down, its eyebrows lift and fall, and its hat rises and falls. A crank is a wheel with a rod attached. When the wheel pushes the rod, you get a sawing action, and when the rod pushes the wheel it turns it around. Cranks turn the wheels of mechanical steam trains.

Machines

WHAT YOU NEED

cardboard box   glue

paper

paints and brush

scissors

tape

wire

pencil

tin foil

1 Paint a scary night-time scene on the cardboard box.

2 Draw and paint a skeleton and ghost and cut them out.

3

Mold the wire into the shape shown and glue on the ghost and skeleton.

4 Poke a hole in each end of the box. Hold the wire above the box and gently insert the ends through the holes. Tape tin foil around both ends of the wire.

You are now ready to make the spooky characters pop up!

27

Weights and pulleys

A tall crane uses pulleys to lift and lower heavy loads at docks or at construction sites. Pulleys allow us to do more work with less effort. A pulley is a long piece of cable wound around a series of grooved wheels, and attached to a heavy object or load. One pulley is useful, but several pulleys make lifting much easier.

Double power

It is easier to pull a heavy object down than it is to push the object up. A pulley allows you to pull down on a cable, instead of pushing up. The more pulley wheels you use, the farther you have to pull the cable, but using less **force**.

A block and tackle is a set of pulleys linked together. It is used at the end of the arm, or jib, of a crane to increase the force of the crane's lifting power.

Lifting and lowering

Tower cranes are fixed in one place, such as a tall building, and the long jib is supported by a tower. A **trolley** runs backward and forward along the jib. A cable runs from the trolley to a powerful **hoist**, worked by an electric motor. Hanging from the trolley is the hook. When the hoist turns, it lifts and lowers the hook. The hook may be carrying a large weight, so there is a **counterweight** at the other end of the jib to keep the tower balanced. Large tower cranes are put up piece by piece. Once the first section is in place, the crane builds itself, lifting and fitting new sections. It uses the push of a **hydraulic ram** to lift itself for the next section. Other types of cranes are built on trucks or wheels and are moved around a construction site.

Machines

Cargo crane

variety of cardboard boxes

glue

paints and brush

cardboard

toothpicks

beads

wire

gold thread

paper fastener

scissors

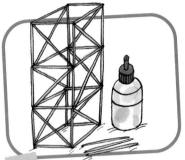

1 Make a tower from toothpicks. Glue a piece of cardboard on top to make a flat roof. Glue onto a box platform.

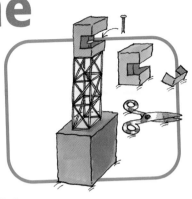

2 Attach a small box cabin to the platform with a paper fastener so the crane can twist. Cut out a window.

3 Cut two pieces of cardboard. Glue toothpicks on one piece, as shown, then glue the other piece on top. Glue this platform onto the cabin to make a swivel arm. Then glue a box to the other end. Paint your crane.

4 Glue three beads along the crane's framework, as shown. Thread a piece of gold thread through the beads. Make a wire hook and attach to one end.

Paint small cargo boxes, stick a wire loop on top of each, and attach to your crane

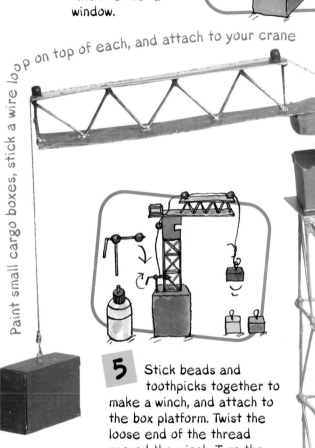

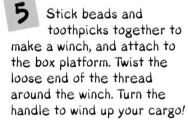

5 Stick beads and toothpicks together to make a winch, and attach to the box platform. Twist the loose end of the thread around the winch. Turn the handle to wind up your cargo!

29

Jet planes

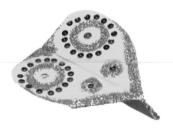

If you blow up a balloon and let it go, the air rushes out and the balloon shoots forward. This is because the balloon has forward **thrust**. To keep going, an airplane also needs forward thrust. In a jet engine, burning fuel produces a hot gas, which rushes out of the back of the engine, thrusting the airplane forward. The airplane's smooth shape also stops backward **drag** from the air. Fighter aircraft are fast, powerful jets.

Spinning blades

A turbojet engine has a turbine, which is a wheel with blades. The turbine turns blades at the front of the engine, sucking in air. The air is heated, and compressed, which means that it is forced into a smaller space. The air escapes out the back of the engine, moving the aircraft forward, in the same way a balloon moves forward when the air is let out of it. Turbojet engines are used to power fast jets, such as the Concorde, but they are very noisy.

Whizzing fans

A turbofan is like a turbojet engine, but with a fan at the front that pushes the air back even more. A turbofan engine gives the jet more thrust, allowing it to take off easier and climb higher. Turbofan engines are used on long-distance aircraft because they are quiet and use very little fuel. Turboprop engines have propellers spun by the **exhaust** gases. They are slower and better for shorter flights.

Machines

WHAT YOU NEED

paper

sequins

glitter

glue

scissors

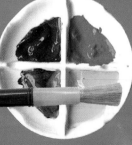
paints and brush

Paper jets

1 Fold a piece of paper in half. Open it up and fold the two edges into the center line to form a triangle out of the front section.

2 Re-fold at the center. Fold the sides down so that you have a plane shape.

Fly your planes outside with your friends – which plane flies the farthest?

3 Make a cut in the bottom and fold it through to form a tail.

4 Glue the center shut. Paint and decorate your plane with sequins.

Experiment with different shapes and colors for your planes.

Wind power

You feel the power of the wind when it blows. Sometimes the wind is so strong it blows trees over. Wind power is a form of energy. It is used to make heat or electricity, or to move things. Two of the earliest uses of wind energy were sailboats and windmills.

Sails in the wind

Windmills are built in many different shapes and sizes, but they all work in the same basic way. They usually have two blades with a paddle-shaped sail at each end, making four sails in all. The sails are shaped so that the wind pushes against them, moving them around and causing the blades to turn.

Energy from air

Windmills, or wind turbines, are built high up on towers so that they catch the stronger winds blowing high above ground. As the blades move, they force a wheel to turn. The wheel is connected to a water pump or an electricity generator which creates an even stronger source of power. Long ago, the power made by windmills was used to grind grain into flour. As the wind blew the blades around, they moved heavy stone **millwheels** which ground the grain between them.

Wind farms

Today, windmills are grouped together in large wind farms. These farms are usually located on coasts or hilltops where it is especially windy.

Machines

WHAT YOU NEED

paintbrush

glue

thin wooden stick

scissors

white paper

cork

paints

pencil

1
Paint a square of paper on both sides in two different colors.

2 When dry, fold the paper along each diagonal and then open it up again.

3
Cut half way toward the center from each corner.

4
Mark four corners with crosses as shown.

5
Fold each marked corner into the center and glue into place.

6 Cut a two inch (5 cm) piece off the wooden stick. Push it through the center of the paper.

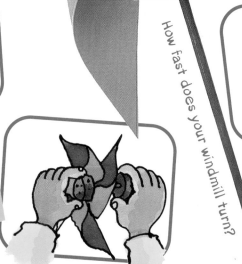

7 Ask an adult to cut a cork in half. Push each half of the cork firmly into each end of the stick.

How fast does your windmill turn?

8
Push the long piece of stick firmly into the cork at the back of your windmill.

33

Blast off!

A rocket has to reach a speed of 25,000 miles (40,000 km) an hour to escape the pull of Earth's **gravity**. A space rocket is mostly made up of engines and fuel. A multi-stage rocket has several engines. Some engines give the rocket a big push to blast off. Other engines drive the rocket through space to its target or help steer it. As each engine finishes its task, it drops off, leaving the rest of the rocket to complete the mission.

Oxygen cargo

The rocket carries all the **oxygen** it needs to burn fuel, because there is no air in space. The first stage of a rocket, such as the American Atlas V, carries more than 31,000 gallons (114,000 L) of oxygen, as well as 16,000 gallons (62,000 L) of **kerosene**. The second stage above it contains all the oxygen and liquid **hydrogen** fuel that the engine needs. There are also tiny engines that are fired to steer the rocket.

Engine drop off

At ignition, the stage of liftoff when the engines are started, the main engines are fired to help provide thrust to lift the rocket off the ground. After a couple of minutes, when their fuel is used up, these engines are jettisoned, or thrown off. The next stage then takes over, using its engines to reach the correct **orbit**. Finally, the payload, or main body of the rocket, is launched and the second stage engine falls away. Space rockets only make one journey. The Space Shuttle is an Orbiter that can make up to a hundred journeys. It rides on the back of a large fuel tank that feeds fuel to its engines, then falls back to Earth.

Machines

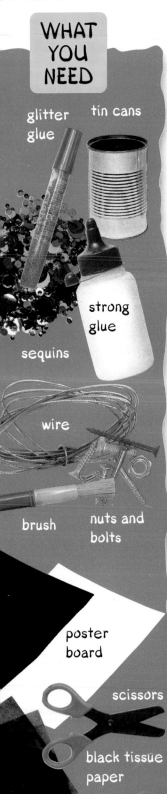

WHAT YOU NEED

glitter glue

tin cans

strong glue

sequins

wire

brush

nuts and bolts

poster board

scissors

black tissue paper

Add constellations by joining up metallic stars with glitter glue

2 Squash two tin cans flat and glue them on the poster board to make the body of the rocket. Cut out two strips of metal and glue to both sides to make the main engines. Add a metal triangle for a nozzle.

1 Glue black tissue paper to poster board.

3 Decorate your rocket. Glue on tin lids for windows. Add metal strips to make sections on the body.

4 Thread sequins onto pieces of wire. Curl the ends so they stay in place. Attach the twisted sparkles to the base of your rocket to look like fire.

Warning:
Ask an adult to help with any sharp edges and with extra strong glue.

35

Power stations

You cannot dig or drill for electricity. It has to be generated, or produced, from a natural energy source such as gas, oil, coal, or nuclear fuel in a **power station**. The energy source is used to spin an **electromagnet** to create electrical energy. Usually, the magnet is spun by a turbine, which is a wheel with blades that turns when water or steam passes through it.

Making steam

Power stations burn fuel to heat water to make steam. Some burn trash, or a product of waste, called Refuse Derived Fuel, or RDF. RDF plants **recycle** trash to make fuel. Some small power stations burn wood or straw for fuel. Another recycling system called coppicing is used to cut wood from trees for fuel, without cutting the whole tree down. Most power stations are wasteful, using only about one-third of the energy from the burning fuel to make electricity. The rest of the energy is lost as heat.

Power savers

Combined-cycle power stations use the waste gases from burning fuel and steam to spin the turbines. These power stations produce up to one-sixth more electricity. Nuclear power stations use fuel from metals, such as uranium or plutonium, to make steam to drive turbines. In a part of the power station called the steel reactor core, the fuel breaks up into tiny particles, producing heat to warm water. The heated water turns to steam to power the turbines.

A power station in California, USA.

Machines

Smoking chimneys

paper

poster
board

pencil

pastels

oil pastels

paints
and
brush

glue

1 Draw an outline of a factory scene, with warehouses, chimneys, and power stations.

2 Use the pastels and paints to color your picture. Smudge the colors with your fingers for a smokey effect.

3 Mount your picture on poster board.

Add busy little toothpick people to your factory scene

Robotics

A robot is a machine that carries out tasks automatically. Robots are controlled by a microchip or computer, which is programmed to do a job. Robots are used for all sorts of jobs, such as building cars or working in space.

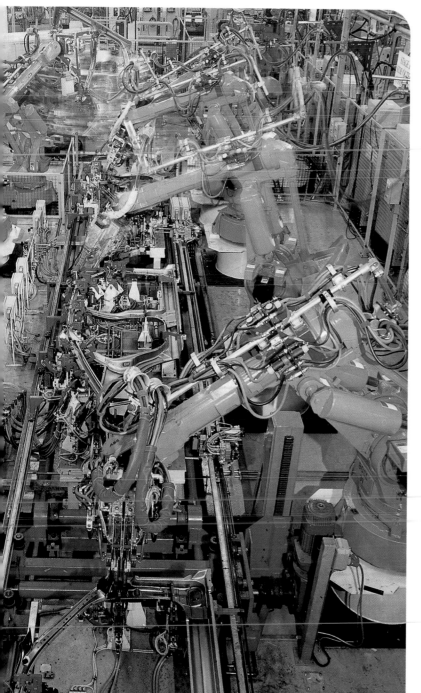

Robotic arms

Many robots are made up of a single arm that can be programmed by a computer to perform different jobs. They are called robotic arms. The arm, top, and base of the robot can all rotate. They can also stretch to reach different points. Robot tools were first used in a Japanese factory in 1970.

Reliable workers

A factory robot carries out simple tasks in a certain order. For example, it will first get the material it has to work on in the right place. It then changes tools and works on the material, such as drilling it, shaping it, or even painting it. The material is then passed along a production line to the next robot. More advanced robot workers use built-in **sensors**, such as cameras, to help them do their jobs. The advantage of using a robot is that it can work in conditions that are dangerous for human workers.

Thinking machines

A robot can be made to learn things just as humans do by using computer programs. For example, a robot can be made to find its way around a maze. The robot can see where it is going and is able to avoid obstacles. In the future, robots that behave and look just like humans may be built. Scientists might even be able to create artificial, or human-made, skin to cover these machines. Robots that look like humans are called androids.

Machines

WHAT YOU NEED

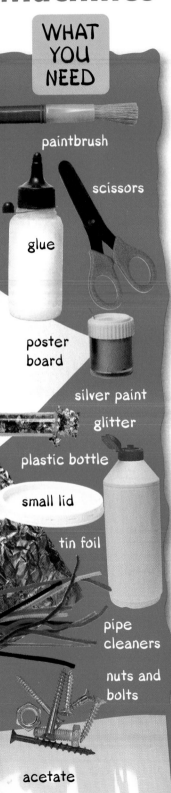

paintbrush

scissors

glue

poster board

silver paint

glitter

plastic bottle

small lid

tin foil

pipe cleaners

nuts and bolts

acetate

Shiny robot

1 Ask an adult to help you cut the top off the bottle.

2 Cut out three panels from one side, and glue acetate in the holes to make windows.

3 Paint the bottle silver. Scatter with glitter before it dries.

4 Using strong glue, stick on bolts, nuts, and foil shapes.

5 Glue bolts and pipe-cleaner circles onto the small lid to make eyes.

6 Cut out circles from poster board and paint them silver. Thread them onto two pipe cleaners.

Poke the pipe-cleaner arms through the sides of your robot. You can bend them into any position!

Decorate your robot with shiny bits and pieces

39

Moon buggy

It takes a very special type of car to travel on the Moon or one of the planets. The American Lunar Roving Vehicle, or Moon buggy, carries astronauts and all their gear on the rocky, dusty surface of the Moon. It folds up in the storage bay of the spacecraft for the journey, then it is unfolded to explore the moon's surface.

Lunar vehicles

The Moon buggy was first used on the Apollo Mission in 1971. Moon buggies have been used on all three manned Moon trips. To avoid punctures, the four tires of the Moon buggy are solid. It is powered by a battery that takes it for a 16-mile (26-km) round trip, at a top speed of 11 miles (18 km) an hour. It is steered by a bar instead of a wheel.

At the back are storage lockers for the tool kit and bags for Moon rock samples. At the front is a camera and an antenna for sending TV pictures back to Earth.

Remote controlled explorers

The Russian Lunokhod was first taken to the Moon by the unmanned spacecraft, Luna 17. Steered from Earth, it visited and sampled several sites, recording and sending back information. In July 1997, the most distant land journey ever was made by NASA's Sojourner Rover, which explored part of the surface of Mars. This tiny vehicle, weighing just over two pounds (1 kg), sent over 500 pictures of the surface of Mars back to Earth. A new, bigger model will stay on Mars for a year, and will take surface samples of the planet.

Machines

Mars lander

cardboard boxes

glue

matches

pencil

poster board

paints and brush

pipe cleaners

tin foil

bubble wrap

1 Create a Mars lander by gluing together a number of boxes.

2 Use pieces of rolled-up poster board to make legs. Glue onto the body of the vehicle.

3 Draw and cut out a circle from poster board. Cut a straight line to the middle of the circle and fold as shown, to form a cone shape for the satellite probe. Glue onto the vehicle.

4 Stick matches onto the end of a pipe cleaner to make an antenna and glue on.

5 Paint your vehicle and decorate it with foil.

Make a planetary landscape for your Mars lander to roam on

Micro-machines

Micro-submarines are being developed to explore inside the human body, looking for problems and even repairing body parts.

A tiny vehicle can find its way to problem areas and take a look, using a miniature camera. It might even be able to do surgery. One day, it may be possible to build computers this size. The microchips will be no bigger than molecules, which are the tiniest pieces of matter. Who knows, we might be able to build a computer as smart as a human brain, and the size of a brain!

Nanotechnology is the science of building micro-machines, or machines as small as four hundred-thousandths of an inch (.001 mm) across. An electric motor attached to a scrap of **silicon** one-fortieth of an inch (.1 mm) wide spins 600,000 times every minute. Its gear wheels are no wider than one of your hairs! It will soon be possible to build a micro-machine that copies itself, producing new machines as they are needed.

How small?

Scientists use a scanning electron microscope to build machines this tiny. This kind of microscope shows and moves single **atoms** and molecules, and can even drill millions of holes in one tiny speck of dust. Electron microscopes can write the words of an entire encyclopedia set on a pinhead!

Insect robots

Computer-controlled insects may soon be able to go into areas which are difficult or too dangerous for humans to enter. Cockroaches with back-pack controls are now being tested in Japan. Micro-robot insects are also being developed in the United States. They could soon be used to check and repair inside machinery.

Repair mission

Scientists are able to build robot machines so tiny that they can travel through the bloodstream to different parts of your body.

Machines

What You Need

glue

empty matchboxes

scissors

paints and brush

beads

cardboard

gold thread

needle

silver foil

toothpicks

pencil

Mini scooter and skateboard

1 Paint and decorate two matchboxes, inside and out.

2 Draw the outline of a skateboard and a scooter on cardboard. Cut out, paint, and decorate.

3 Cut up toothpicks into small pieces, long enough to fit across the width of the scooter and skateboard platforms. Bind them together with gold thread, as shown.

Make other mini-machines that fit into a matchbox

Make a handlebar for the scooter with toothpicks. Poke a hole in the top of the platform and insert the handlebar.

4 Thread a bead on each end and secure them by gluing on small balls of foil.

5 Make two holes in the bottom of each platform to insert the sets of wheels.

Future cars

The first cars were noisy, smoky, and used a lot of fuel. Modern cars go farther on less fuel, and produce less **pollution**. Most automobiles use gasoline, or gas, for fuel, but they still produce waste gases that cause pollution. To reduce environmental damage, car manufacturers are looking for new ways to power their products.

Battery power

Some electric cars exist, but even they cause pollution. This is because the electricity they use is generated, or produced, at a fuel-burning power station. Electric cars have very heavy batteries, which do not hold enough power for a long journey. Electric vehicles are ideal for delivery vans and short trips.

Best of both

A hybrid car uses gas and electricity together. Its gasoline engine not only drives the car, but also runs a generator. This produces electricity and charges the car's batteries. When driving around town, the car runs on its electric motor. On a longer journey, the gas engine gives extra power. Whenever the brakes are applied, a heavy **flywheel** starts spinning. The spinning flywheel turns the generator, storing extra energy in the batteries.

Future fuels?

Car makers are working on cars powered by the Sun's energy. They run on hundreds of **solar cells**, but are very expensive to produce. Experiments are also being carried out with hydrogen fuel cells, because hydrogen gives off very little pollution. There are problems with using hydrogen because it is a flammable and explosive gas.

The solar-powered racing car Sunraycer, manufactured by General Motors.

Transportation

Designer vehicles

glue

paints and brush

pencil

scissors

poster board

graph paper

1 Draw several future cars on graph paper. Paint and cut them out.

2 Paint a border around a large piece of graph paper and glue on your cars.

3 Mount your picture on poster board.

Draw other forms of future transportation - buses, ships, planes, and space modules

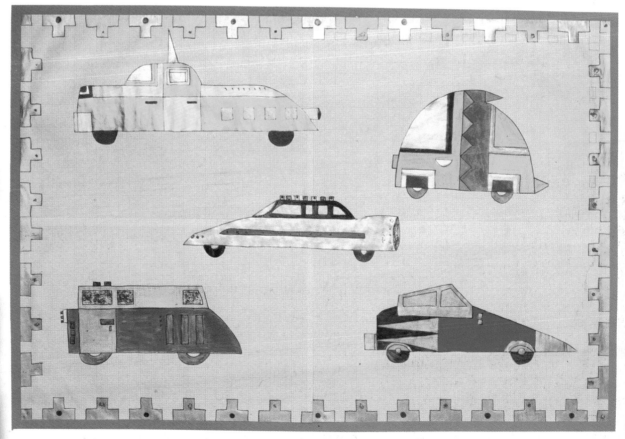

Glossary

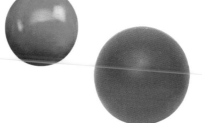

aluminum A light, strong material used to make many kinds of vehicles.

atom The smallest unit of an element.

counterweight A weight used to keep a machine balanced.

damper A small block wrapped in felt that is used in a piano to stop the wires from vibrating.

digital Presenting information in the form of digits.

drag The force that works opposite to thrust. Drag pulls back on an object.

electricity A form of energy used to power such things as lights, televisions, and other appliances. Electricity is both found in nature and made by humans.

electric motors Machines that get energy from wires carrying electricity or from batteries. Electric motors are quiet and do not produce waste gases.

electromagnet A piece of iron that turns into a magnet when an electric current passes through a coil wrapped around the iron.

engineering The science of building roads, bridges, and buildings.

escapement The part of a mechanical watch that controls the speed at which the spring and weight are released.

exhaust The waste gases, caused by burning fuel, escaping from an engine.

filter A part in a synthesizer that changes the shape of a sound wave, changing the way it sounds.

flywheel A rotating wheel used to slow down the speed and revolutions of another machine part.

force A push or a pull. Forces work in pairs.

friction A force that slows down an object when it comes in contact with another object.

gas engines Gas engines work by burning a combination of gasoline and air in a cylinder. The heat from the ignited gasoline forces down the piston in the cylinder and causes wheels to turn.

gears Wheels with teeth that fit together. When one wheel turns, it catches on another wheel and forces it to turn too.

generator A machine that makes electricity.

gravity The natural force that pulls objects to Earth.

gyroscope An instrument that is made up of a spinning wheel resting on an axis. When the wheel turns, the instrument balances on its axis. A spinning top is an example of a gyroscope.

hoist The part of a crane that the cable is wrapped around. When the cable is wound around the hoist using a crank, the hook holding the heavy object is raised or lowered.

hydraulic ram A machine that uses the force of liquid pressure to move objects up and down.

hydrogen A colorless, flammable gas.

kerosene A light colored oil used as a fuel.

lever A bar balanced on a point called a fulcrum. Force pushing on one end of the bar can raise a weight on the other end of the bar.

mast A tall pole on ships from which the sail hangs.

microchip A very tiny piece of silicon that carries electricity. It is used in computers and watches.

millwheel A wheel, powered by water, that supplies power.

molecule The most basic unit of matter.

note The combination of the pitch, or highness or lowness, and tone of a sound.

nuclear reactor The area of a nuclear power station where heat is made from uranium or plutonium fuel.

orbit To move around something.

overtone A higher tone produced with the original tone.

oxygen A colorless, odorless gas.

perpetual Describes something that lasts forever.

pollution Waste materials that damage our planet.

power station A place where electricity is produced from an energy source, such as coal or nuclear fuel.

printing press A machine that prints by pressing paper against an ink covered surface.

quartz A clear, hard mineral found in rocks.

recycle To take materials from trash for reuse.

reel A device that is used for winding.

resistance A force that slows the movement of an object.

rod and crank A rod, or long straight bar, attached to a wheel, or crank. When the rod moves back and forth, the wheel turns around.

sensors Parts of a machine, such as a robot, that collect information and help it do its work.

silicon A chemical used to make microchips.

solar cells Panels of silicon that collect the sun's energy.

spring A coil-shaped wire that keeps its shape after being stretched or squashed.

sprocket A wheel with tooth-like projections.

steam-powered Driven by steam.

streamlined A shape designed to move as fast as possible through air or water.

synthesizer An instrument that produces an electronic sound.

thrust A force that moves an object forward.

trolley An electrically operated device that runs along a track.

turbine A motor driven by water, gas, wind, or other kinds of energy to produce electricity.

turning shaft A rod or bar which is part of a machine and can rotate.

Index

47

Materials guide

A list of materials, how to use them, and suitable alternatives

The crafts in this book require the use of materials and products that are easily purchased in craft stores. If you cannot locate some materials, you can substitute other materials with those we have listed here, or use your imagination to make the craft with what you have on hand.

Gold foil: can be found in craft stores. It is very delicate and sometimes tears.

Silver foil: can be found in craft stores. It is very delicate, soft, and sometimes tears. For some crafts, tin or aluminum foil can be substituted. Aluminum foil is a less delicate material and makes a harder finished craft.

PVA glue: commonly called polyvinyl acetate. It is a modeling glue that creates a type of varnish when mixed with water. It is also used as a strong glue. In some crafts, other strong glues can be substituted, and used as an adhesive, but not as a varnish.

Filler paste: sometimes called plaster of Paris. It is a paste that hardens when it dries. It can be purchased at craft and hardware stores.

Paste: a paste of 1/2 cup flour, one tablespoon of salt and one cup of warm water can be made to paste strips of newspaper as in a papier mâché craft. Alternatively, wallpaper paste can be purchased and mixed as per directions on the package.

Cellophane: a clear or colored plastic material. Acetate can also be used in crafts that call for this material. Acetate is a clear, or colored, thin plastic that can be found in craft stores.

WHAT YOU NEED

gold foil

silver foil

filler paste

PVA glue

flour

salt

cellophane or acetate

1 2 3 4 5 6 7 8 9 0   Printed in the USA   0 9 8 7 6 5 4 3 2